Science Around You
Fizz in the Kitchen

Susan Martineau
illustrated by Leighton Noyes

with thanks to Kathryn Higgins,
Head of Chemistry, Leighton Park School

contents

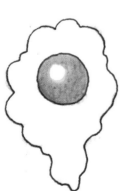

How to be a Scientist

Scientists learn about the world around us by doing experiments.
You will learn about the science in your kitchen in this book.
You won't need any special equipment for these experiments.
You'll probably find most of it in your kitchen already.
Don't forget to ask a grown-up first before using it.
Before you begin, always read through the whole
experiment to make sure you have everything you need.

BE SAFE!
Ask a grown-up
to stand by –
especially when
you are heating or
cutting things.

Bubble Trouble!

Fizzy drinks have loads of bubbles in them. These bubbles are made of a gas that has been mixed into the liquid. You can have some fun with these bubbles. Clear fizzy drink is better than cola so that you can see what it happening.

1. Put some lemonade or clear fizzy drink into a glass.

2. Drop a handful of raisins into the liquid.

3. Watch what happens to the raisins.

Let's Take a Closer Look!

The bubbles of GAS in the drink stick to the raisins. The GAS is lighter than the LIQUID and so it rises to the top of the glass, carrying the raisins with it. The bubbles then pop and the raisins sink back down. But more bubbles stick to them and up they go again!

Did You Know?

Other food also has gas bubbles in it. The holes inside fairy cakes, muffins and breads are made by gas bubbles too.

Quick Quizzer!

Can you find out the name of this gas?

Clue: look on page 7.

The Big Fizz

Stand by for some bubbling fun with this experiment. You need to stand the glass in a shallow dish or the sink to catch any overflowing froth. Please don't put your face too near the glass as the fizz is very stinky!

1. Put 1 tablespoon of baking powder in a large glass.

2. Stand the glass inside a dish.

3. Put 2 tablespoons of vinegar into a small jug.

4. Pour the vinegar into the baking powder.

Let's Take a Closer Look!

The baking powder and the vinegar are different types of chemicals. When they are mixed something called a CHEMICAL REACTION happens. The reaction makes a GAS called CARBON DIOXIDE that causes all the bubbling and fizzing.

Wash everything down the sink afterwards.

Try This!

Use a funnel to put some baking powder inside a balloon. Put some vinegar in a small bottle and carefully put the balloon over the neck. Watch the balloon blow up as the powder and vinegar react.

Quick Warning!

Make sure you don't get the vinegar near your eyes or it will sting.

Air Power

Trick your friends with this experiment.
No one will believe that it will work.
All you need is the kitchen sink, a plastic beaker,
some kitchen towel and the air around you!

1. Push the kitchen towel firmly into the bottom of the beaker.

2. Fill the sink with water.

3. Turn the beaker upside down. Hold it straight and push it down into the water.

4. Count to ten. Lift the beaker straight out without tipping it.

Did You Know?

The air around us is a mixture of gases. The main ones are called NITROGEN and OXYGEN. Most gases are invisible but they take up space just like the air in your beaker.

Let's Take a Closer Look!

Amazingly the paper towel does not get wet. No water gets into the beaker because the beaker is already full of air. You cannot see it but it is taking up space inside the beaker so that the water cannot get in.

Quick Fact

Some gases are very smelly. One, called hydrogen sulphide, smells of bad eggs!

Oily Stuff

Oil and water do not mix. If you try to mix oil with water you will see that when you stop stirring the oil stays on the top, or surface, of the water. But if you add some washing-up liquid to the water something very interesting happens.

1. Pour some water into a bowl.

2. Add some cooking oil.

3. Now add some drops of washing-up liquid and stir the water.

When was the last time you did the washing-up?

Did You Know?

Birds have a sort of oil smeared on their feathers. It keeps them waterproof so that they don't get soaking wet in the rain or on a pond.

Quick Fact!

Oil from oil tankers sometimes spills into the seas and oceans. This oil is very bad for sea birds. It floats on the top of the water and can kill them and other sea creatures.

Get those greasy dishes clean with some washing-up liquid!

Let's Take a Closer Look!

The drops of oil float on top of the water. They have a kind of stretchy skin around them and they like to stick together. The washing-up liquid breaks up the skin and helps to mix the oil and water together.

Waterworks

When you turn on the tap out comes
clean water for drinking, cooking and washing.
Before it reaches us water has to be cleaned,
or filtered, to get rid of bugs and dirt. We can
make a water filter to clean out some dirt.
Just push the kitchen towel into the funnel.
Use a sieve if you haven't got a funnel.

1. Mix some soil and water in a jug.

2. Put a piece of kitchen towel into a funnel.

3. Hold the funnel over another jug and slowly pour the dirty water into it.

Let's Take a Closer Look!

The kitchen towel acts as a FILTER. It lets the water through but stops most of the soil and dirt. Our drinking water is filtered through gravel and sand at water treatment works to get rid of dirt. Chemicals are also added to the filtered water to kill any harmful germs that might make us ill.

Try This!

Water is precious so don't waste it. Remember to turn off the tap when you are cleaning your teeth!

Quick Warning!

Don't drink your filtered water. You can use it to water the garden or house plants.

Many people in the world can't just turn on the tap like us.

They have to walk miles to fetch clean water.

Slimes Around You

Every liquid in the kitchen has its own different stickiness. If you try stirring a jar of water it is easier than stirring a jar of very sticky syrup. We can do a stickiness test on some liquids to see which is the stickiest one of all! You'll need some water, syrup, vegetable oil and washing-up liquid.

1. Find four identical plastic beakers. Pour a different liquid into each one to the same level.

2. Ask a friend to help. You each need two marbles.

3. Drop a marble into each beaker at the same time and from the same height.

4. Watch how long each one takes to reach the bottom of the beaker.

Let's Take a Closer Look!

The stickiness of a LIQUID, or how runny it is, is called VISCOSITY. Thick, gooey LIQUIDS have high VISCOSITY and it is hard to make things move through them, like marbles or spoons. Thin and runny LIQUIDS, like water, have low VISCOSITY. The marble moves quickly through them.

Have you tried swimming through syrup!

Did You Know?

The companies that make sauces like ketchup have to make sure the viscosity is just right or the sauce will either stick in the bottle or come out too quickly!

Quick Quizzer!

Do you think that milk has lower or higher viscosity than syrup?

Ketchup Coins

Make your pocket money coins look shiny and new with this experiment. Ketchup in a squeezy bottle is ideal but, if yours isn't in a squeezy bottle, you can just dollop some ketchup into a small bowl and use a spoon instead.

1. Put some dirty copper coins on a plate.

2. Squeeze or dollop a small amount of ketchup on to each one.

3. Leave the coins for about an hour.

4. Rinse off the ketchup.

Ask your friends and family if you can borrow coins from them if you haven't any of your own.

Try This!

Take one large copper coin. Use a cocktail stick to put tiny blobs of ketchup on the coin to make eyes and a mouth. Leave and then rinse off for a smiley ketchup coin!

Let's Take a Closer Look!

Copper coins get dirty and dull-looking. The ketchup has vinegar in it. Vinegar is something called an ACID. It is this ACID that reacts with the dirty coating on the coin, leaving it nice and shiny.

Quick Fact!

Lemons taste sharp because they have acid in them.

Mouldy Matters

You'll need two slices of bread and two chunks of cheese for this experiment but you won't be making sandwiches with it. We're going to find out why some food needs to be kept cool.

1. Seal each slice of bread and each chunk of cheese in four separate plastic bags.

2. Put a bag of bread and a bag of cheese in the fridge. Put the other two on the windowsill.

3. Check them each day and draw or keep a note of what happens to the bread and cheese.

Did You Know?

Food stored in a freezer can keep for several months. Put a piece of cheese and a piece of bread in the freezer and you will be able to eat a cheese sandwich when you are hungry in a few months' time!

Quick Warning!

Never put plastic bags near your face. Throw away the mouldy bagfuls.

I can't have a snack if it's kept in the fridge!

Quick Quizzer!

In hot weather do you think the bread and cheese will go mouldy more or less quickly?

Let's Take a Closer Look!

The bread and cheese on the windowsill start growing blue-green MOULD after a few days. MOULD grows on things that are no longer fresh. Food does not go off so quickly in very cold places, like the fridge. Mould does not like the cold.

Melting Moments

When we are cooking – heating, chopping, mixing and stirring – we are really doing experiments. This one is very tasty too! First of all, you need to find some small cakes or biscuits and a bar of chocolate.

1. Break up the chocolate and put it in a bowl over a pan of gently simmering water.

2. Stir it well as it becomes all runny and hot.

3. Spoon some chocolate sauce on to each cake or biscuit.

Let's Take a Closer Look!

The chocolate chunks start as SOLID. As you heat them up they change, or MELT, and become a LIQUID. When you spoon this LIQUID on to the cakes or biscuits it cools down and becomes SOLID again.

Try This!

Try and think of how other foods change when you heat them or they get warm. You could keep a note of the changes or draw them.

Quick Warning!

Ask a grown-up to help when you are melting the chocolate.

Always use oven gloves to hold hot things like the bowl of chocolate.

Quick Quizzer!

What happens to solid ice when it heats up?

Stretchy Eggs

You'll end up with a nice pudding when you've done this experiment! It is a little bit tricky separating the egg yolks from the whites but it is useful to know how to do this. Use the yolks to make an omelette later. Ask a grown-up to help with the oven.

1. Put two egg whites into a bowl.

2. Whisk them with a hand or electric whisk until they stand up in stiff points.

3. Whisk in 50 g caster sugar. Gently stir in another 50 g sugar.

4. Spoon six large blobs on to baking parchment on a baking tray. Put in the oven for 2 ¹/₂ hours at 100°C/200°F.

Try This!

Serve your meringues with strawberries and cream!

That's four for me and two for you.

Quick Tip!

To separate the egg yolk from the white, break the egg in half. Slide the yolk from one half to the other and let the white dollop down into a bowl.

Let's Take a Closer Look!

Whisking the egg whites traps air inside them. The CELLS that the egg whites are made of stretch because of this air and they grow bigger or EXPAND. When the frothy white mixture is heated in the oven it hardens into a tasty meringue!

Words to Know

Acid – Acids have a very sour taste. Vinegar and lemon juice are acid liquids.

Carbon Dioxide – Carbon dioxide is a gas. It is the gas that is put into fizzy drinks to make the fizz. It is also the gas our bodies breathe out into the air.

Cells – Every single living thing in the world is made up of loads and loads of tiny parts called cells.

Chemical Reaction – This is when two or more chemicals are mixed together and they change and make something new.

Expand – To expand means to spread out or get bigger.

Filter – A filter is a way of separating solids from a liquid.

Gas – The air around us is a mixture of different gases, like oxygen and nitrogen. A gas does not have a shape of its own.

Liquid – Water is a liquid. Liquids can be poured and do not have a shape of their own.

Melt – when a solid is heated and turns into a liquid we say it has melted.

Mould – Mould is a very small sort of fungus. It grows on things that are going bad.

Nitrogen – Nitrogen is a gas in the air around us.

Oxygen – Oxygen is a gas in the air around us. It is the gas we need to breathe to stay alive.

Solid – Solid things, like blocks of ice or chocolate, have a shape of their own.

Viscosity – This is a way of measuring how sticky or runny liquids are.

Quizzer Answers

Page 5 – carbon dioxide

Page 9 – oxygen

Page 15 – lower

Page 19 – if it isn't in the fridge, food will go off more quickly.

Page 21 – it melts and becomes liquid in the form of water.